More BIBLE SONGS to Tunes You Know

Daphna Flegal

Abingdon Press
Nashville

How to Use This Songbook

Music is a fun and effective way to teach young children. The rhythmic patterns and repetiton help children remember Bible verses, the names of Bible people, and Bible stories. Music can help with classroom management. Songs can call the children to the story time, tell children it's time to clean up, and help children quiet themselves for prayer. Music also offers children the opportunity to move and "get the wiggles out." It's one way children who learn kinetically (through movement) can have successful learning experiences.

But what if you:

- Only sing in the shower?
- Don't read music?
- Don't like to sing in front of others?

Then this songbook has more songs for you!

More Bible Songs to Tunes You Know is filled with many more songs to use with young children to help them learn about the Bible. Each song uses a familiar tune, such as "London Bridge" or "Twinkle, Twinkle, Little Star" so that the songs are easy for you and your children to sing together. The tune is listed under the title of the song.

Just in case you do read music, the melody line for each tune is printed in the back of the songbook along with guitar chords. The tunes are in their common form. You may need to modify the song's melody and rhythm to make the words fit the notes. To help you fit the words to the melody, we have underlined the portions of the words that fall on the strong beats of the melody.

Remember, children don't care if you are a great singer. They just want to sing. So pick a tune, sing a song, and "make a joyful noise!"

MORE BIBLE SONGS TO TUNES YOU KNOW

Copyright © 2001 by Abingdon Press

This book is printed on acid-free, recycled paper.

ISBN 978-0-687-05840-2

07 08 09 10 — 10 9 8 7 6 5 4 3 2

MANUFACTURED IN THE UNITED STATES OF AMERICA

Contents

The Bible

The Bible Is Its Name-O
(Tune: Bingo)

Oh, here's the book we love to read;
The Bible is its name-o.
B-I-B-L-E,
B-I-B-L-E,
B-I-B-L-E,
The Bible is its name-o.

Oh, here's the book we love to read;
The Bible is its name-o.
(clap)-I-B-L-E,
(clap)-I-B-L-E,
(clap)-I-B-L-E,
The Bible is its name-o.

Oh, here's the book we love to read;
The Bible is its name-o.
(clap)-(clap)-B-L-E,
(clap)-(clap)-B-L-E,
(clap)-(clap)-B-L-E,
The Bible is its name-o.

Oh, here's the book we love to read;
The Bible is its name-o.
(clap)-(clap)-(clap)-L-E,
(clap)-(clap)-(clap)-L-E,
(clap)-(clap)-(clap)-L-E,
The Bible is its name-o.

Oh, here's the book we love to read;
The Bible is its name-o.
(clap)-(clap)-(clap)-(clap)-E,
(clap)-(clap)-(clap)-(clap)-E,
(clap)-(clap)-(clap)-(clap)-E,
The Bible is its name-o.

Oh, here's the book we love to read;
The Bible is its name-o.
(clap)-(clap)-(clap)-(clap)-(clap),
(clap)-(clap)-(clap)-(clap)-(clap),
(clap)-(clap)-(clap)-(clap)-(clap),
The Bible is its name-o.

Oh, here's the book we love to read;
The Bible is its name-o.
B-I-B-L-E,
B-I-B-L-E,
B-I-B-L-E,
The Bible is its name-o.

Words: Pam Snider
Words © 2001 Abingdon Press

The Bible Is the Word of God
(Tune: Mary Had a Little Lamb)

The Bible is the Word of God,
Word of God, Word of God.
The Bible is the Word of God,
And God's Word is true.

Based on Psalm 33:4 (Good News Bible)
Words: Daphna Flegal
Words © 2001 Abingdon Press

Say Our Verse
(Tune: Row, Row, Row Your Boat)

Say, say, say our verse,
Say our verse right now.
Stand up tall and say it all;
I know you know how.

Words: Daphna Flegal
Words © 2001 Abingdon Press

Time to Get Together
(Tune: The More We Get Together)

It's time to get together, together, together.
It's time to get together and listen right
    now.
'Cause we'll hear a story that's found in the
    Bible,
It's time to get together and listen right
    now.

Words: Daphna Flegal
Words © 2001 Abingdon Press

Bible Times

If I Lived in Bible Times
(Tune: Do You Know the Muffin Man?)

If I lived in Bible times,
Bible times, in Bible times,
If I lived in Bible times,
I'd have a family.

If I lived in Bible times,
Bible times, in Bible times,
If I lived in Bible times,
I'd have a house of mud.

If I lived in Bible times,
Bible times, in Bible times,
If I lived in Bible times,
I would bake my bread.

If I lived in Bible times,
Bible times, in Bible times,
If I lived in Bible times,
I would learn and grow.

Words: Cynthia Gray, Linda Ray Miller, and Fran Porter
Words © 2001 Cokesbury

Bible Times Work and Play
(Tune: This Is the Way)

This is the way we sweep the floor,
(Pretend to sweep.)
Sweep the floor, sweep the floor.
This is the way we sweep the floor,
In our house of mud.

This is the way we roll the roof,
(Pretend to push a roller back and forth.)
Roll the roof, roll the roof.
This is the way we roll the roof,
In our house of mud.

This is the way we carry water,
(Pretend to hold a jar of water on your head.)
Carry water, carry water.
This is the way we carry water,
In our house of mud.

This is the way we shoo the chickens,
(Pretend to wave your hands at chickens.)
Shoo the chickens, shoo the chickens.
This is the way we shoo the chickens,
In our house of mud.

This is the way we light the lamp,
(Pretend to light an oil lamp.)
Light the lamp, light the lamp.
This is the way we light the lamp,
In our house of mud.

This is the way we climb the stairs,
(Pretend to climb stairs.)
Climb the stairs, climb the stairs.
This is the way we climb the stairs,
In our house of mud.

This is the way we pray at home,
(Fold hands in prayer.)
Pray at home, pray at home.
This is the way we pray at home,
In our house of mud.

Words: Cynthia Gray, Linda Ray Miller, and Fran Porter
Words © 2001 Cokesbury

If I Lived Long, Long, Ago
(Tune: Twinkle, Twinkle, Little Star)

If I lived long, long ago,
These are things that I would know.
I'd know how to watch the sheep,
And unroll my mat to sleep.
If I lived long, long ago,
These are things that I would know.

If I lived long, long ago,
These are things that I would know.
I'd know how to bake the bread,
And how Hebrew words were read.
If I lived long, long ago,
These are things that I would know.

If I lived long, long ago,
These are things that I would know.
I'd know how to farm and fish,
And to make a potter's dish.
If I lived long, long ago,
These are things that I would know.

If I lived long, long ago,
These are things that I would know.
I'd know how to say a prayer,
Thanking God for all God's care.
If I lived long, long ago,
These are things that I would know.

Words: Daphna Flegal
Words © 2001 Abingdon Press

Creation

And God Saw That It Was Good
(Tune: The Farmer in the Dell)

God saw that it was good. (clap, clap)
God saw that it was good. (clap, clap)
God made the sun and moon and stars,
And saw that it was good. (clap, clap)

God saw that it was good. (clap, clap)
God saw that it was good. (clap, clap)
God made the sky and sea and earth,
And saw that it was good. (clap, clap)

God saw that it was good. (clap, clap)
God saw that it was good. (clap, clap)
God made the seeds and plants and trees,
And saw that it was good. (clap, clap)

God saw that it was good. (clap, clap)
God saw that it was good. (clap, clap)
God made the fish and birds and cows,
And saw that it was good. (clap, clap)

God saw that it was good. (clap, clap)
God saw that it was good. (clap, clap)
God made me and God made you,
And saw that it was good. (clap, clap)

Based on Genesis 1
Words: Daphna Flegal
Words © 2000 Cokesbury

God Made
(Tune: God Is So Good)

God made the sun.
God made the moon.
God made the stars,
And God saw it was good!

God made the sky.
God made the earth.
God made the sea,
And God saw it was good!

God made the seeds.
God made the plants.
God made the trees,
And God saw it was good!

God made the *(have a child say an animal)*.
God made the *(have the next child say an animal)*.
God made the *(have the next child say an animal)*,
And God saw it was good!

God made us all.
God made us all.
God made us all,
And God saw it was good!

Based on Genesis 1
Words: Lora Jean Gowan, Cynthia Gray,
and Doug Meyer
Words © 2000 Cokesbury

God Gives Us the Things We Need
(Tune: London Bridge)

God gives us the things we need,
Things we need, things we need.
God gives us the things we need,
Things like *(Let the children name something from God's world)*.

Based on Genesis 1
Words: Daphna Flegal
Words © 1998 Abingdon Press

Do You Know God Made the Moon?
(Tune: Do You Know the Muffin Man?)

Do you know God made the moon,
Made the moon, made the moon?
Do you know God made the moon,
And saw that it was good?

Yes, we know God made the moon,
Made the moon, made the moon.
Yes, we know God made the moon,
And saw that it was good.

Do you know God made the stars,
Made the stars, made the stars?
Do you know God made the stars,
And saw that it was good?

Yes, we know God made the stars,
Made the stars, made the stars.
Yes, we know God made the stars,
And saw that it was good.

(Let the children name other things from God's world.)

Based on Genesis 1
Words: Daphna Flegal
Words © 1999 Abingdon Press

People Parade
(Tune: The Wheels on the Bus)

Our God made people everywhere,
Everywhere, everywhere.
Our God made people everywhere,
And saw that it was good.

Our God made people run, run, run!
Run, run, run! Run, run, run!
Our God made people run, run, run!
And saw that it was good.

Our God made people hop, hop, hop!
Hop, hop, hop! Hop, hop, hop!
Our God made people hop, hop, hop!
And saw that it was good.

Our God made people tip, tip, toe!
Tip, tip, toe! Tip, tip, toe!
Our God made people tip, tip, toe!
And saw that it was good.

Our God made people shake, shake, shake!
Shake, shake, shake! Shake, shake, shake!
Our God made people shake, shake, shake!
And saw that it was good.

Our God made people everywhere,
Everywhere, everywhere.
Our God made people everywhere.
And saw that it was good.

Based on Genesis 1:26-27
Words: Daphna Flegal
Words © 2000 Cokesbury

Noah

On Noah's Ark
(Tune: Down by the Bay)

On Noah's ark
All the animals stay;
Down in the dark
Is where they play.
And if you look,
Old Noah will say,
"Did you ever see a bear
With curly hair,
On No-ah's ark."

On Noah's ark
All the animals stay;
Down in the dark
Is where they play.
And if you look,
Old Noah will say,
"Did you ever see a pig
Dancing a jig,
On No-ah's ark."

On Noah's ark
All the animals stay;
Down in the dark
Is where they play.
And if you look,
Old Noah will say,
"Did you ever see a snail
Chasing its tail,
On No-ah's ark."
(Let the children make up additional rhymes.)

Based on Genesis 6:14; 17-22
Words: Daphna and Gary Flegal
Words © 2001 Abingdon Press

Old Man Noah
(Tune: Twinkle, Twinkle, Little Star)

Old man Noah built an ark;
Made it out of hickory bark.
Brought the animals two by two,
Elephants and kangaroos.
Old man Noah built an ark;
Made it out of hickory bark.

Based on Genesis 6:14; 17-22
Words: Daphna and Diana Flegal
Words © 2001 Abingdon Press

A Man Named Noah
(Tune: Old MacDonald)

A man named Noah built an ark,
'Cause God told him so.
And on this ark he had two ducks,
'Cause God told him so.
With a quack, quack, here,
And a quack, quack, there,
Here a quack, there a quack,
Everywhere a quack, quack.
Noah built a great big ark,
'Cause God told him so.

A man named Noah built an ark,
'Cause God told him so.
And on this ark he had two cows,
'Cause God told him so.
With a moo, moo, here,
And a moo, moo, there,
Here a moo, there a moo,
Everywhere a moo, moo.
Noah built a great big ark,
'Cause God told him so.

A man named Noah built an ark,
'Cause God told him so.
And on this ark he had two dogs,
'Cause God told him so.
With a woof, woof, here,
And a woof, woof, there,
Here a woof, there a woof,
Everywhere a woof, woof.
Noah built a great big ark,
'Cause God told him so.

A man named Noah built an ark,
'Cause God told him so.
And on this ark he had two pigs,
'Cause God told him so.
With an oink, oink, here,
And an oink, oink, there,
Here an oink, there an oink,
Everywhere an oink, oink.
Noah built a great big ark,
'Cause God told him so.

Based on Genesis 6:14; 17-22
Words: Lora Jean Gowan, Cynthia Gray, and Doug Meyer
Words © 2000 Cokesbury

Two Itsy Bitsy Spiders
(Tune: The Itsy Bitsy Spider)   T-Th

Two itsy bitsy spiders
(Use fingers to make a pretend spider.)
Climbed into Noah's boat.
(Cup hands to make boat.)
Down came the rain
*(Hold hands up above head; then bring
hands down while wiggling fingers.)*
And set the boat afloat.
(Wave hands to indicate water.)
Up came the sun
(Hold hands in a circle above head.)
And dried up all the rain.
*(Move hands down; then bring hands up
while wiggling fingers.)*
And two itsy bitsy spiders
(Use fingers to make pretend spiders.)
Climbed down the boat again.
(Cup hands to make boat.)

Two fuzzy wuzzy rabbits
(Use fingers to make rabbit ears.)
Climbed into Noah's boat.
(Cup hands to make boat.)
Down came the rain
*(Hold hands up above head; then bring
hands down while wiggling fingers.)*
And set the boat afloat.
(Wave hands to indicate water.)
Up came the sun
(Hold hands in a circle above head.)
And dried up all the rain.
*(Move hands down; then bring hands up
while wiggling fingers.)*
And two fuzzy wuzzy rabbits
(Use fingers to make rabbit ears.)
Climbed down the boat again.
(Cup hands to make boat.)

Two roly poly puppies
(Use hands to make puppy ears.)
Climbed into Noah's boat.
(Cup hands to make boat.)
Down came the rain
*(Hold hands up above head; then bring
hands down while wiggling fingers.)*

And set the boat afloat.
(Wave hands to indicate water.)
Up came the sun
(Hold hands in a circle above head.)
And dried up all the rain.
*(Move hands down; then bring hands up
while wiggling fingers.)*
And two roly poly puppies
(Use hands to make puppy ears.)
Climbed down the boat again.
(Cup hands to make boat.)

Two teeny weeny inch worms
(Wiggle index finger.)
Climbed into Noah's boat.
(Cup hands to make boat.)
Down came the rain
*(Hold hands up above head; then bring
hands down while wiggling fingers.)*
And set the boat afloat.
(Wave hands to indicate water.)
Up came the sun
(Hold hands in a circle above head.)
And dried up all the rain.
*(Move hands down; then bring hands up
while wiggling fingers.)*
And two teeny weeny inch worms
(Wiggle index finger.)
Climbed down the boat again.
(Cup hands to make boat.)

Based on Genesis 6:14; 17-22
Words: Daphna Flegal
Words © 2001 Abingdon Press

See a Rainbow
(Tune: Twinkle, Twinkle, Little Star)   m

See a rainbow in the sky;
See the colors passing by.
Red and yellow, green and blue,
Show us God loves me and you.
See a rainbow in the sky;
See the colors passing by.

Based on Genesis 9:13
Words: Daphna Flegal
Words © 2001 Abingdon Press

See the Rainbow
(Tune: Are You Sleeping?)

See the rainbow,
See the rainbow,
Way up high,
Way up high,
Telling of God's promise,
Telling of God's promise,
In the sky,
In the sky.

Based on Genesis 9:13
Words: Daphna Flegal
Words © 2001 Abingdon Press

The Animals on Noah's Ark
(Tune: This Is the Way)

This is the way the rabbits hopped,
(Hop like a rabbit.)
Rabbits hopped, rabbits hopped.
This is the way the rabbits hopped
To get on Noah's ark.

This is the way the lizards creeped,
(Creep on tiptoes.)
Lizards creeped, lizards creeped.
This is the way the lizards creeped
To get on Noah's ark.

This is the way the eagles flew,
(Flap arms like wings.)
Eagles flew, eagles flew.
This is the way the eagles flew
To get on Noah's ark.

This is the way the elephants stomped,
(Stomp; swing arm like a trunk.)
Elephants stomped, elephants stomped.
This is the way the elephants stomped
To get on Noah's ark.

This is the way the horses pranced,
(Step high.)
Horses pranced, horses pranced.
This is the way the horses pranced
To get on Noah's ark.

This is the way the turtles crawled,
(Crawl or step slowly.)
Turtles crawled, turtles crawled.
This is the way the turtles crawled
To get on Noah's ark.
(Let the children think of other animals and motions.)

Based on Genesis 6:14; 17-22
Words: Daphna Flegal
Words © 2001 Abingdon Press

Abraham, Sarah, Jacob, Joseph

Go, Abraham
(Tune: Hot Cross Buns)

Go, go, go!
God said, "Go!
Leave your home and family, and
Go, go, go."

Here, here, here.
God said, "Here:
Here's the land I'll give your children.
Here, here, here."

Count, count, count.
God said, "Count.
Count the stars if you can count them.
Count, count, count."

Family, family,
You'll have lots of people in your
Family.

Based on Genesis 12:1-9; 15:1-6
Words: Sharilyn S. Adair
Words © 2000 Abingdon Press

God Is with Me
(Tune: Are You Sleeping?)

God is with me.
God is with me.
Every day, every day.
Monday, Tuesday, Wednesday,
Thursday, Friday, Saturday,
Sunday too, here with you.

Based on Genesis 28:15
Words: Beth Parr and Pam Snider
Words © 2001 Abingdon Press

11

Do You Know That God Is Here?
(Tune: Do You Know the Muffin Man?)

Do you know that God is here,
God is here, God is here?
Do you know that God is here,
And with us all the time?

(Child's name) knows that God is here,
God is here, God is here.
(Child's name) knows that God is here,
And with us all the time.

Based on Genesis 28:15
Words: Beth Parr and Pam Snider
Words © 1998 Abingdon Press

God Called Abraham
(Tune: Are You Sleeping?)

God called Abraham,
God called Abraham,
"Go this way,
Go this way,
To a land I show you,
To a land I show you.
Go today,
Go today."

Based on Genesis 12:1-4
Words: Daphna Flegal
Words © 2001 Abingdon Press

Sarah Laughed
(Tune: Hot Cross Buns)

Sarah laughed.
Sarah laughed.
When she heard the strangers speaking,
Sarah laughed.

Sarah laughed.
Sarah laughed.
When she had the promised baby,
Sarah laughed.

Sarah laughed.
Sarah laughed.
When she named the baby Isaac,
Sarah laughed.

Based on Genesis 18:1-15
Words: Daphna Flegal
Words © 2001 Abingdon Press

Jacob Had a Dream
(Tune: The Farmer in the Dell)

Oh, Jacob had a dream,
(Fold hands together on one side of your head, as if sleeping.)
Oh, Jacob had a dream.
As he slept upon the ground,
(Touch the ground.)
Oh, Jacob had a dream.
(Fold hands together on one side of your head, as if sleeping.)

Oh, Jacob had a dream,
(Fold hands on one side of your head.)
Oh, Jacob had a dream.
He saw a ladder reach to heav'n,
(Stretch arms up high over your head.)
Oh, Jacob had a dream.
(Fold hands on one side of your head.)

Oh, Jacob had a dream,
(Fold hands on one side of your head.)
Oh, Jacob had a dream.
There were angels on the ladder.
(Wave arms like angel wings.)
Oh, Jacob had a dream.
(Fold hands on one side of your head.)

Oh, Jacob had a dream,
(Fold hands on one side of your head.)
Oh, Jacob had a dream.
God spoke to Jacob in the dream.
(Shake index finger.)
Oh, Jacob had a dream.
(Fold hands on one side of your head.)

Oh, Jacob had a dream,
(Fold hands on one side of your head.)
Oh, Jacob had a dream.
God said, "I will be with you."
(Point to self.)
Oh, Jacob had a dream.
(Fold hands on one side of your head.)

Based on Genesis 28:10-15
Words: Daphna Flegal
Words © 2001 Abingdon Press

When Jacob Gave Joseph a New Coat
(Tune: My Bonnie Lies over the Ocean)

When Jacob gave Joseph a new coat,
A new coat with colors so bright,
It made all the brothers so jealous,
That soon there would be a big fight.
Joseph, Joseph,
Your new coat has colors so bright, so bright.
Joseph, Joseph,
Your new coat has colors so bright.

The brothers sent Joseph to Egypt
Right after the terrible fight.
But God was with Joseph in Egypt,
And everything turned out all right.
Joseph, Joseph,
Everything turned out all right, all right.
Joseph, Joseph,
Everything turned out all right.

Based on Genesis 37:3-4, 28; 45:4-15
Words: Daphna Flegal
Words © 2001 Abingdon Press

Moses

Down by the River Nile
(Tune: Down by the Riverside)

His mother made him a basket boat,
Down by the river Nile,
Down by the river Nile,
Down by the river Nile.
His mother made him a basket boat,
Down by the river Nile,
Down by the river Nile.

His mother put him inside the boat,
Down by the river Nile,
Down by the river Nile,
Down by the river Nile.
His mother put him inside the boat,
Down by the river Nile,
Down by the river Nile.

His sister watched him in the basket boat,
Down by the river Nile,
Down by the river Nile,
Down by the river Nile.
His sister watched him in the basket boat,
Down by the river Nile,
Down by the river Nile.

The princess found him inside the boat,
Down by the river Nile,
Down by the river Nile,
Down by the river Nile.
The princess found him inside the boat,
Down by the river Nile,
Down by the river Nile.

Based on Exodus 2:1-10
Words: Daphna Flegal
Words © 2001 Abingdon Press

Moses Heard God
(Tune: London Bridge)

Moses saw a burning bush,
Burning bush, burning bush.
Moses saw a burning bush,
On the mountain.

Moses, you're on holy ground,
Holy ground, holy ground.
Moses, you're on holy ground.
Take off your sandals.

Moses heard God say to him,
Say to him, say to him;
Moses heard God say to him,
Free my people.

Moses said I cannot go,
Cannot go, cannot go;
Moses said I cannot go,
Speak to Pharaoh.

God said I will go with you,
Go with you, go with you;
God said I will go with you,
Free my people.

Based on Exodus 3:1-12
Words: Daphna Flegal
Words © 2001 Abingdon Press

Moses Led the People 'Cross the Sea
(Tune: She'll Be Coming 'Round the Mountain)

Oh, Moses led the people 'cross the sea.
Oh, Moses led the people 'cross the sea.
When the sea just up and parted,
When the sea just up and parted,
Oh, Moses led the people 'cross the sea.

Oh, Miriam sang and danced her praise to God.
Oh, Miriam sang and danced her praise to God.
When they made it out of Egypt,
When they made it out of Egypt,
Oh, Miriam sang and danced her praise to God.

Based on Exodus 14:1-25; 15:20-21
Words: Daphna Flegal
Words © 2001 Abingdon Press

He'll Be Coming Down the Mountain
(Tune: She'll Be Coming 'Round the Mountain)

He'll be coming down the mountain with ten laws.
He'll be coming down the mountain with ten laws.
They are called the ten commandments.
They are called the ten commandments.
He'll be coming down the mountain with ten laws.

And these laws help us all know how to live.
And these laws help us all know how to live.
They are called the ten commandments.
They are called the ten commandments.
And these laws help us all know how to live.

Based on Exodus 20:1-17
Words: Daphna Flegal
Words © 2001 Abingdon Press

Love the Lord
(Tune: Row, Row, Row Your Boat)

Love, love, love the Lord.
Love the Lord your God,
With all your heart and soul and might.
Love the Lord your God.

Based on Deuteronomy 6:5
Words: Daphna Flegal
Words © 2001 Abingdon Press

M-O-S-E-S
(Tune: Bingo)

There was a leader called by God
To go and free God's people.
M-O-S-E-S,
M-O-S-E-S,
M-O-S-E-S,
Oh, Moses freed God's people.

There was a leader called by God
To go and free God's people.
(clap)-O-S-E-S,
(clap)-O-S-E-S,
(clap)-O-S-E-S,
Oh, Moses freed God's people.

There was a leader called by God
To go and free God's people.
(clap)-(clap)-S-E-S,
(clap)-(clap)-S-E-S,
(clap)-(clap)-S-E-S,
Oh, Moses freed God's people.

There was a leader called by God
To go and free God's people.
(clap)-(clap)-(clap)-E-S,
(clap)-(clap)-(clap)-E-S,
(clap)-(clap)-(clap)-E-S,
Oh, Moses freed God's people.

There was a leader called by God
To go and free God's people.
(clap)-(clap)-(clap)-(clap)-S,
(clap)-(clap)-(clap)-(clap)-S,
(clap)-(clap)-(clap)-(clap)-S,
Oh, Moses freed God's people.

There was a leader called by God
To go and free God's people.
(clap)-(clap)-(clap)-(clap)-(clap),
(clap)-(clap)-(clap)-(clap)-(clap),
(clap)-(clap)-(clap)-(clap)-(clap),
Oh, Moses freed God's people.

There was a leader called by God
To go and free God's people.
M-O-S-E-S,
M-O-S-E-S,
M-O-S-E-S,
Oh, Moses freed God's people.

Based on Exodus 3:1-12
Words: Daphna and Diana Flegal
Words © 2001 Abingdon Press

Joshua

All Around the City
(Tune: This Is the Way)

This is the way we march around,
(March around the circle.)
March around, march around.
This is the way we march around,
All around the city.

This is the way we blow the trumpets,
(Cup hands around mouth.)
Blow the trumpets, blow the trumpets.
This is the way we blow the trumpets,
All around the city.

This is the way we shout and yell,
(Shake fists in the air.)
Shout and yell, shout and yell.
This is the way we shout and yell,
All around the city.

This is the way the walls fall down,
(Bring hands over head; shake hands and bring down to the floor.)
Walls fall down, walls fall down.
This is the way the walls fall down,
All around the city.

Based on Joshua 6
Words: Daphna Flegal
Words © 2001 Abingdon Press

We Will Serve the Lord
(Tune: The Farmer in the Dell)

We will serve the Lord,
We will serve the Lord,
As for me and my household,
We will serve the Lord.

Based on Joshua 24:15
Words: Daphna Flegal
Words © 2001 Abingdon Press

All 'Round Ol' Jericho
(Tune: Down by the Riverside)

We're gonna march 'round the city walls,
All 'round ol' Jericho,
All 'round ol' Jericho,
All 'round ol' Jericho.
We're gonna march 'round the city walls,
All 'round ol' Jericho,
All 'round ol' Jericho.

We're gonna blow on our trumpets there,
All 'round ol' Jericho,
All 'round ol' Jericho,
All 'round ol' Jericho.
We're gonna blow on our trumpets there,
All 'round ol' Jericho,
All 'round ol' Jericho.

We're gonna shout out with a great shout,
All 'round ol' Jericho,
All 'round ol' Jericho,
All 'round ol' Jericho.
We're gonna shout out with a great shout,
All 'round ol' Jericho,
All 'round ol' Jericho.

We're gonna watch those walls come tumblin' down,
All 'round ol' Jericho,
All 'round ol' Jericho,
All 'round ol' Jericho.
We're gonna watch those walls come tumblin' down,
All 'round ol' Jericho,
All 'round ol' Jericho.

Based on Joshua 6
Words: Daphna Flegal
Words © 2001 Abingdon Press

Ruth, Hannah, Samuel

Ruth
(Tune: London Bridge)

"Where you're going, I will go,
I will go, I will go.
Where you're going, I will go,"
Said Ruth to Naomi.

The women went to Bethlehem,
Bethlehem, Bethlehem.
The women went to Bethlehem,
It was Naomi's home.

Ruth gathered grain to make their bread,
Make their bread, make their bread.
Ruth gathered grain to make their bread,
From grain left in the fields.

Ruth met Boaz in the fields,
In the fields, in the fields.
Ruth met Boaz in the fields
As she gathered grain.

Boaz and Ruth were married then,
Married then, married then.
Boaz and Ruth were married then.
It made Naomi glad.

Soon Ruth had a baby boy,
Baby boy, baby boy.
Soon Ruth had a baby boy,
God blessed this family.

Based on the Book of Ruth
Words: Daphna Flegal
Words © 2001 Abingdon Press

Hannah Said a Prayer
(Tune: Mary Had a Little Lamb)

Hannah said a prayer to God,
Prayer to God, prayer to God.
Hannah said a prayer to God,
To ask God for a son.

Hannah had a baby boy,
Baby boy, baby boy.
Hannah had a baby boy.
She named him Samuel.

Samuel grew and served the Lord,
Served the Lord, served the Lord.
Samuel grew and served the Lord,
As long as Samuel lived.

Based on 1 Samuel 1
Words: Daphna Flegal
Words © 2001 Abingdon Press

A Voice Called in the Night
(Tune: The Farmer in the Dell)

A voice called in the night.
A voice called in the night.
Samuel, O Samuel,
A voice called in the night.

Samuel ran to see.
Samuel ran to see.
He thought Eli called his name,
So Samuel ran to see.

It was the voice of God,
It was the voice of God.
Eli said, "It was not me,"
It was the voice of God.

Here I am, O Lord.
Here I am, O Lord.
I am listening to your word.
Here I am, O Lord.

Based on 1 Samuel 3:1-10
Words: Daphna Flegal
Words © 2001 Abingdon Press

David

Who Watches over You?
(Tune: Baa, Baa, Black Sheep)

Baa, baa, black sheep,
Who watches over you?
Shepherd boy, David,
He is true.
He keeps me safe
From the wolf and the bear.
He finds green pastures;
I eat my fill there.
Baa, baa, black sheep,
Who watches over you?
Shepherd boy, David.
He is true.

Baa, baa, white sheep,
Who watches over you?
Shepherd boy, David,
He is true.
He keeps me safe
From the wolf and the bear.
He finds green pastures;
I eat my fill there.
Baa, baa, white sheep,
Who watches over you?
Shepherd boy, David,
He is true.

Based on 1 Samuel 17:14-15
Words: Daphna Flegal
Words © 2001 Abingdon Press

The Shepherd David Had Some Sheep
(Tune: Old MacDonald)

The Shepherd David had some sheep,
Down in Bethlehem.
He watched those sheep both day and night,
Down in Bethlehem.
With a baa, baa here, and a baa, baa there;
Here a baa, there a baa,
Ev'rywhere a baa, baa.
The Shepherd David had some sheep,
Down in Bethlehem.

The Shepherd David played the harp,
Down in Bethlehem.
He played the harp both day and night,
Down in Bethlehem.

With a plink, plink here, and a plink, plink there;
Here a plink, there a plink,
Ev'rywhere a plink, plink.
A baa, baa here, and a baa, baa there;
Here a baa, there a baa,
Ev'rywhere a baa, baa.
The Shepherd David played the harp.
Down in Bethlehem.

Based on 1 Samuel 16:14-23; 17:14-15
Words: Daphna Flegal
Words © 2001 Abingdon Press

Shepherd Boy
(Tune: This Old Man)

Shepherd boy, shepherd boy,
David was a shepherd boy.
He watched his sheep
While singing songs of joy.
David was a shepherd boy.

Based on 1 Samuel 17:14-15
Words: Daphna Flegal
Words © 2001 Abingdon Press

David Was a Little Shepherd Boy
(Tune: She'll Be Coming 'Round the Mountain)

Oh, David was a little shepherd boy,
Oh, David was a little shepherd boy.
When he fought the great big giant,
When he fought the great big giant,
Oh, David was a little shepherd boy.

Based on 1 Samuel 17:19-58
Words: Daphna Flegal
Words © 2001 Abingdon Press

Abigail
(Tune: This Old Man)

Abigail, Abigail,
The Bible tells of Abigail.
She fed David and all of his men.
And a fight came to an end.

Based on 1 Samuel 25:2-43
Words: Daphna Flegal
Words © 2001 Abingdon Press

Psalms

Come and Praise the Lord
(Tune: Old MacDonald)

All things breathing praise the Lord,
Come and praise the Lord!
Praise the Lord with trumpet sound.
Come and praise the Lord!
With a toot, toot here,
And a toot, toot there;
Here a toot, there a toot,
Ev'rywhere a toot, toot.
All things breathing praise the Lord,
Come and praise the Lord!

All things breathing praise the Lord,
Come and praise the Lord!
Praise the Lord with lute and harp.
Come and praise the Lord!
With a pluck, pluck here,
And a pluck, pluck there;
Here a pluck, there a pluck,
Ev'rywhere a pluck, pluck.
A toot, toot here,
And a toot, toot there;
Here a toot, there a toot,
Ev'rywhere a toot, toot.
All things breathing praise the Lord,
Come and praise the Lord!

All things breathing praise the Lord,
Come and praise the Lord!
Praise the Lord with tambourine.
Come and praise the Lord!
With a shake, shake here,
And a shake, shake there;
Here a shake, there a shake,
Ev'rywhere a shake, shake.
A pluck, pluck here,
And a pluck, pluck there;
Here a pluck, there a pluck,
Ev'rywhere a pluck, pluck.
A toot, toot here,
And a toot, toot there;
Here a toot, there a toot,
Ev'rywhere a toot, toot.
All things breathing praise the Lord,
Come and praise the Lord!

All things breathing praise the Lord,
Come and praise the Lord!
Praise the Lord with flute and pipe.

Come and praise the Lord!
With a twee, twee here,
And a twee, twee there;
Here a twee, there a twee,
Ev'rywhere a twee, twee.
A shake, shake here,
And a shake, shake there;
Here a shake, there a shake,
Ev'rywhere a shake, shake.
A pluck, pluck here,
And a pluck, pluck there;
Here a pluck, there a pluck,
Ev'rywhere a pluck, pluck.
A toot, toot here,
And a toot, toot there;
Here a toot, there a toot,
Ev'rywhere a toot, toot.
All things breathing praise the Lord,
Come and praise the Lord!

All things breathing praise the Lord,
Come and praise the Lord!
Let's praise the Lord with clanging cymbals.
Come and praise the Lord!
With a clang, clang here,
And a clang, clang there;
Here a clang, there a clang,
Ev'rywhere a clang, clang.
A twee, twee here,
And a twee, twee there;
Here a twee, there a twee,
Ev'rywhere a twee, twee.
A shake, shake here,
And a shake, shake there;
Here a shake, there a shake,
Ev'rywhere a shake, shake.
A pluck, pluck here,
And a pluck, pluck there;
Here a pluck, there a pluck,
Ev'rywhere a pluck, pluck.
A toot, toot here,
And a toot, toot there;
Here a toot, there a toot,
Ev'rywhere a toot, toot.
All things breathing praise the Lord,
Come and praise the Lord!

Based on Psalm 150
Words: Daphna Flegal
Words © 2001 Abingdon Press

Lord, Our Lord
(Tune: Hot Cross Buns)

Lord, our Lord,
Lord, our Lord,
How majestic is your name
In all the earth.

Based on Psalm 8
Words: Daphna Flegal
Words © 2001 Abingdon Press

Praise God's Name
(Tune: Three Blind Mice)

Praise God's name.
Praise God's name.
God's holy name.
God's holy name.
Share all your moments in all your days
By lifting your voices in songs of praise.
The God of Creation is here always.
So praise God's name.

Based on Psalm 145:2
Words: Daphna and Gary Flegal
Words © 2001 Abingdon Press

Sing, Sing, Sing
(Tune: Row, Row, Row Your Boat)

Sing, sing, sing your praise;
Sing new songs of joy.
Lift your voices in a song,
Every girl and boy.

Based on Psalm 149:1
Words: Daphna and Gary Flegal
Words © 2001 Abingdon Press

Songs of Joy
(Tune: Are You Sleeping?)

Hear us singing, hear us singing,
Songs of joy, songs of joy.
Let all things now living
Praise God with thanksgiving.
Sing God's praise.
Sing God's praise.

Based on Psalm 147:7
Words: Daphna and Gary Flegal
Words © 2001 Abingdon Press

Note: "Praise God's Name," "Sing, Sing, Sing," and "Songs of Joy" may be sung as a praise medley. Divide the group into three sections. Begin by having section 1 sing "Praise God's Name." Then have section 2 sing "Sing, Sing, Sing." Finally have section 3 sing "Songs of Joy."

I'll Give Thanks
(Tune: Three Blind Mice)

I'll give thanks,
I'll give thanks,
Unto the Lord,
Unto the Lord.
I'll tell of all your wonderful deeds.
I will sing praise unto your name.
The Lord Most High
The Lord Most High

Based on Psalm 9
Words: Daphna Flegal
Words © 2001 Abingdon Press

The Prophets

Jeremiah's Call
(Tune: Do You Know the Muffin Man?)

Jeremiah heard God's call,
He heard God's call, he heard God's call.
Jeremiah heard God's call.
He said, "I am too small."

God said, "I will be with you,
Will be with you, will be with you."
God said, "I will be with you.
No, you're not too small."

We can tell of God's great love,
Of God's great love, of God's great love.
We can tell of God's great love,
For we are not too small.

Based on Jeremiah 1:1-9
Words: Beth Parr
Words © 2001 Abingdon Press

Amos Was a Prophet
(Tune: I'm a Little Teapot)

Amos was a prophet all his days,
He told the people to live God's way.
He wanted all the people to hear him say,
"Do good for others everyday."

I can be a prophet all my days,
I can do my best to live God's way.
I can be like Amos, I can say,
"Do good for others everyday."

Based on Amos 5:1-27
Words: Daphna Flegal
Words © 2001 Abingdon Press

Build the Wall
(Tune: Are You Sleeping?)

Nehemiah, Nehemiah,
Build the wall, build the wall.
Build it 'round the city,
Build it 'round the city,
Tall and strong.
Tall and strong.

Based on Nehemiah 1:1–2:20
Words: Daphna Flegal
Words © 2001 Abingdon Press

Elijah
(Tune: She'll Be Coming 'Round the Mountain)

Oh, Elijah was a prophet for the Lord.
Oh, Elijah was a prophet for the Lord.
Oh, Elijah was a prophet; oh, Elijah was a prophet;
Oh, Elijah was a prophet for the Lord.

Oh, Elijah won a contest for the Lord.
Oh, Elijah won a contest for the Lord.
Oh, Elijah won a contest; oh, Elijah won a contest;
Oh, Elijah won a contest for the Lord.

Oh, Elijah built an altar to the Lord.
Oh, Elijah built an altar to the Lord.
Oh, Elijah built an altar; oh, Elijah built an altar;
Oh, Elijah built an altar to the Lord.

Based on 1 Kings 18:1-39
Words: Daphna Flegal
Words © 2001 Abingdon Press

Esther, Daniel, Jonah

Anywhere and Anytime
(Tune: The Farmer in the Dell)

Oh, Hannah prayed to God.
Oh, Hannah prayed to God.
At the temple at Shiloh,
Oh, Hannah prayed to God.

Oh, Esther prayed to God.
Oh, Esther prayed to God.
When she went to see the king,
Oh, Esther prayed to God.

Oh, Daniel prayed to God.
Oh, Daniel prayed to God.
From the hungry lions' den,
Oh, Daniel prayed to God.

Oh, Jonah prayed to God.
Oh, Jonah prayed to God.
From the belly of a fish,
Oh, Jonah prayed to God.

Oh, we can pray to God.
Oh, we can pray to God.
Anywhere and anytime,
Oh, we can pray to God.

Based on 1 Samuel 1:1-18; Esther 5:1-8; Daniel 6:19-24; and Jonah 2:1-10
Words: Daphna Flegal
Words © 2001 Abingdon Press

Down in the Den

(Tune: The Wheels on the Bus)

The law of the king says pray to me,
Pray to me, pray to me.
The law of the king says pray to me,
Or you will die.

But Daniel says, "No! I pray to God,
Pray to God, pray to God."
But Daniel says, "No! I pray to God,
Three times a day."

So Daniel is thrown down in the den,
In the den, in the den.
So Daniel is thrown down in the den,
Down in the den.

The lions in the den go, "roar, roar, roar,
Roar, roar, roar, roar, roar, roar."
The lions in the den go, "roar, roar, roar,"
Down in the den.

Oh, hear Daniel pray, "Please help me,
God,"
"Help me, God, Help me, God."
Oh, hear Daniel pray, "Please help me,
God,"
Down in the den.

The lions in the den go, "snore, snore,
snore,
Snore, snore, snore, snore, snore, snore."
The lions in the den go, "snore, snore,
snore,"
Down in the den.

So Daniel is brought up from the den,
From the den, from the den.
So Daniel is brought up from the den,
Up from the den.

The king tells the people to pray to God,
Pray to God, pray to God.
The king tells the people to pray to God,
The living God.

Based on Daniel 6:1-26
Words: Daphna Flegal
Words © 2001 Abingdon Press

Jonah, Won't You Go?

(Tune: I've Been Workin' on the Railroad)

Jonah, won't you go to Ninevah,
Ninevah today?
Jonah, God wants you to go there,
Don't you try to run away.

If you take a boat to Tarshish,
The winds and the waves are gonna blow.
You'll be swallowed by a big fish,
Jonah, won't you go?

Jonah won't you go,
Jonah won't you go,
Jonah won't you go to Ninevah?

Jonah won't you go,
Jonah won't you go,
Jonah won't you go, go, go?

Someone's got a message for Jonah,
Someone's got a message I know.
Someone's got a message for Jonah,
Sayin' Jonah won't you go?
And singing fee fi fiddly i o,
Fee fi fiddly i o, fee fi fiddly i o,
Sayin' Jonah won't you go?

Based on the Book of Jonah
Words: Daphna Flegal
Words © 2001 Abingdon Press

Queen Esther

(Tune: Hot Cross Buns)

Queen Esther,
Queen Esther,
She was brave and saved her people.
Queen Esther.

Based on the Book of Esther
Words: Daphna Flegal
Words © 2001 Abingdon Press

Jesus Is Born!

Let's Get Ready
(Tune: Are You Sleeping?)

Let's get ready,
Let's get ready
To hear good news,
To hear good news:
An angel came to Mary.
An angel came to Mary.
Tell good news.
Tell good news.

Let's get ready,
Let's get ready
To hear good news,
To hear good news:
Go with us to Bethlehem,
Go with us to Bethlehem.
Tell good news.
Tell good news.

Let's get ready,
Let's get ready
To hear good news,
To hear good news:
Welcome baby Jesus,
Welcome baby Jesus.
Tell good news.
Tell good news.

Let's get ready,
Let's get ready
To hear good news,
To hear good news:
The shepherds saw the baby,
The shepherds saw the baby.
Tell good news.
Tell good news.

Let's get ready,
Let's get ready
To hear good news,
To hear good news
Wise men saw the bright star,
Wise men saw the bright star.
Tell good news.
Tell good news.

Based on Luke 1:26-38; Luke 2:1-20; and Matthew 2:1-12
Words: Fran Porter, Cynthia Gray, and Linda Ray Miller
Words © 2000 Cokesbury

Good News
(Tune: London Bridge)

I am bringing you good news,
You good news, you good news.
I am bringing you good news
of great joy.

Based on Luke 2:10
Words: Fran Porter, Cynthia Gray, and Linda Ray Miller
Words © 2000 Cokesbury

We Can Tell the Good News to Our Friends
(Tune: She'll Be Coming 'Round the Mountain)

Oh, yes, we can tell the good news to our friends.
Oh, yes, we can tell the good news to our friends.
Oh, yes, we can tell the good news.
We can tell the good news.
Oh, yes, we can tell the good news to our friends.

Based on Luke 1:26-28
Words: Daphna Flegal
Words © 1997 Abingdon Press

Name Him Jesus
(Tune: Did You Ever See a Lassie?)

You will name the baby Jesus,
The angel told Mary.
You will name the baby Jesus,
For he is God's Son.

Based on Luke 1:31
Words: Daphna Flegal
Words © 1997 Abingdon Press

You   name   Jesus

The Kind Old Innkeeper
(Tune: Old MacDonald)

The <u>K</u>ind Inn<u>k</u>eeper <u>h</u>ad a <u>s</u>table,
<u>O</u>n that <u>s</u>tarry <u>n</u>ight.
And <u>i</u>n that <u>s</u>table he <u>h</u>ad a <u>d</u>onkey,
<u>O</u>n that <u>s</u>tarry <u>n</u>ight.
With a <u>h</u>ee haw <u>h</u>ere, and a <u>h</u>ee haw
there;
<u>H</u>ere a <u>h</u>ee, there a <u>h</u>aw,
<u>E</u>'vrywhere a <u>h</u>ee haw.
The <u>K</u>ind Inn<u>k</u>eeper <u>h</u>ad a <u>s</u>table,
<u>O</u>n that <u>s</u>tarry <u>n</u>ight.

The <u>K</u>ind Inn<u>k</u>eeper <u>h</u>ad a <u>s</u>table,
<u>O</u>n that <u>s</u>tarry <u>n</u>ight.
And <u>i</u>n that <u>s</u>table he <u>h</u>ad a (*Name an ani-mal.*),
<u>O</u>n that <u>s</u>tarry <u>n</u>ight.
With a (*animal sound*) <u>h</u>ere, and a (*animal sound*) <u>t</u>here;
<u>H</u>ere a (*animal sound*), <u>t</u>here a (*animal sound*),
<u>E</u>'vrywhere a (*animal sound*).
The <u>K</u>ind Inn<u>k</u>eeper <u>h</u>ad a <u>s</u>table,
<u>O</u>n that <u>s</u>tarry <u>n</u>ight.

(Let the children name different animals to include in the song.)

Based on Luke 2:1-7
Words: Daphna Flegal
Words © 1997 Abingdon Press

Stable Song
(Tune: In a Cabin in a Wood)

<u>L</u>ittle <u>s</u>table <u>i</u>n the <u>t</u>own,
(Make a tent overhead with hands, finger-tips touching.)
<u>B</u>right star<u>l</u>ight is <u>s</u>hining <u>d</u>own.
(Hold both hands up, fingers outstretched. Wiggle fingers as you bring the arms down.)
<u>T</u>iny <u>b</u>aby, <u>G</u>od's own <u>S</u>on,
(Pretend to rock a baby.)
<u>J</u>esus <u>i</u>s the <u>O</u>ne.
(Hold up index finger.)

Based on Luke 2:1-7
Words: LeeDell Stickler
Words © 1999 Abingdon Press

Hear the Bells Ring
(Tune: Are You Sleeping?)

<u>H</u>ear the <u>b</u>ells ring,
<u>H</u>ear the <u>b</u>ells ring.
<u>D</u>ing dong <u>d</u>ing.
<u>D</u>ing dong <u>d</u>ing.
<u>T</u>elling us it's <u>C</u>hristmas,
<u>T</u>elling us it's <u>C</u>hristmas.
<u>D</u>ing dong <u>d</u>ing.
<u>D</u>ing dong <u>d</u>ing.

(Let the children ring bells as you sing together.)

Words: Daphna Flegal
Words © 1998 Abingdon Press

The Animals Were in the Stable
(Tune: The Farmer in the Dell)

The <u>a</u>nimals were in the <u>s</u>table.
The <u>a</u>nimals were in the <u>s</u>table.
<u>O</u>n that special <u>C</u>hristmas <u>n</u>ight
The <u>a</u>nimals were in the <u>s</u>table.

The <u>d</u>onkey <u>w</u>alked like <u>t</u>his.
The <u>d</u>onkey <u>w</u>alked like <u>t</u>his.
<u>O</u>n that special <u>C</u>hristmas <u>n</u>ight
The <u>d</u>onkey <u>w</u>alked like <u>t</u>his.

The <u>c</u>ow <u>w</u>alked like <u>t</u>his.
The <u>c</u>ow <u>w</u>alked like <u>t</u>his.
<u>O</u>n that special <u>C</u>hristmas <u>n</u>ight
The <u>c</u>ow <u>w</u>alked like <u>t</u>his.

The <u>s</u>heep <u>w</u>alked like <u>t</u>his.
The <u>s</u>heep <u>w</u>alked like <u>t</u>his.
<u>O</u>n that special <u>C</u>hristmas <u>n</u>ight
The <u>s</u>heep <u>w</u>alked like <u>t</u>his.

The <u>d</u>ove <u>f</u>lew like <u>t</u>his.
The <u>d</u>ove <u>f</u>lew like <u>t</u>his.
<u>O</u>n that special <u>C</u>hristmas <u>n</u>ight
The <u>d</u>ove <u>f</u>lew like <u>t</u>his.

The <u>a</u>nimals <u>s</u>aw the <u>b</u>aby.
The <u>a</u>nimals <u>s</u>aw the <u>b</u>aby.
<u>O</u>n that special <u>C</u>hristmas <u>n</u>ight
The <u>a</u>nimals <u>s</u>aw the <u>b</u>aby.

(Encourage the children to move like the animals named in the song.)

Based on Luke 2: 1-7
Words: Daphna Flegal
Words © 1999 Abingdon Press

See the Shepherds
(Tune: Mary Had a Little Lamb)

See the shepherds watch their sheep,
Watch their sheep, watch their sheep.
See the shepherds watch their sheep
On this Christmas night.

See the angels in the sky,
In the sky, in the sky.
See the angels in the sky
On this Christmas night.

Hear the angels tell good news,
Tell good news, tell good news.
Hear the angels tell good news
On this Christmas night.

A Savior now is born for you,
Born for you, born for you.
A Savior now is born for you,
On this Christmas night.

Hurry, shepherds, go and see,
Go and see, go and see.
Hurry, shepherds, go and see
On this Christmas night.

See the baby sleeping there,
Sleeping there, sleeping there.
See the baby sleeping there
On this Christmas night.

Hear the shepherds praising God,
Praising God, praising God.
Hear the shepherds praising God
On this Christmas night.

Based on Luke 2:8-20
Words: Daphna Flegal
Words © 2001 Abingdon Press

Praise with Simeon and Anna
(Tune: This Is the Way)

This is the way we go to the temple,
(March in place.)
Go to the temple, go to the temple.
This is the way we go to the temple,
And thank God for Jesus.
(Clap hands and turn around.)

This is the way we see the baby,
(Make glasses with hands.)
See the baby, see the baby.
This is the way we see the baby,
And thank God for Jesus.
(Clap hands and turn around.)

This is the way we hold the baby,
(Pretend to rock baby.)
Hold the baby, hold the baby.
This is the way we hold the baby,
And thank God for Jesus.
(Clap hands and turn around.)

This is the way we show our praise,
(Shake hands above head.)
Show our praise, show our praise.
This is the way we show our praise,
And thank God for Jesus.
(Clap hands and turn around.)

Based on Luke 2:22-38
Words: Daphna Flegal
Words © 1998 Abingdon Press

Twinkle, Twinkle, Shining Star
(Tune: Twinkle, Twinkle, Little Star)

Twinkle, twinkle, shining star,
We are wise men from afar,
Following a star so bright,
Looking for a king this night.
Twinkle, twinkle, shining star,
We are wise men from afar.

Based on Matthew 2:1-11
Words: Daphna Flegal
Words © 1998 Abingdon Press

Three Wise Men
(Tune: Hot Cross Buns)

Three wise men
Three wise men
Searching for a king by starlight
Three wise men

Three wise men
Three wise men
Bringing gifts to honor Jesus
Three wise men

Based on Matthew 2:1-12
Words: Daphna Flegal
Words © 2001 Abingdon Press

Shining Star
(Tune: This Old Man)

Shining star, shining star,
Shine to show us where you are.

Shine your light on little Bethlehem.
Guide the path of the wise men.

Based on Matthew 2:1-12
Words: Daphna Flegal
Words © 2001 Abingdon Press

The Boy Jesus

Jesus Grew
(Tune: Here We Go 'Round the Mulberry Bush)

I was small, *(Crouch down to appear small.)*
But now I'm tall. *(Stand up straight.)*
I was small, *(Crouch down.)*
But now I'm tall. *(Stand up.)*
I was small, *(Crouch down.)*
But now I'm tall. *(Stand up.)*
Jesus grew! I did too! *(Point to self.)*

Based on Luke 2:40
Words: Cynthia Gray
Words © 2000 Cokesbury

Here Is Jesus in the Temple
(Tune: Did You Ever See a Lassie?)

Here is Jesus in the Temple,
The Temple, the Temple.
Here is Jesus in the Temple,
With teachers around.
He's teaching and learning.
He's teaching and learning.
Here is Jesus in the Temple,
With teachers around.

Based on Luke 2:41-52
Words: Daphna and Gary Flegal
Words © 2001 Abingdon Press

Baby Jesus Grew
(Tune: The Farmer in the Dell)

Oh, Baby Jesus grew.
Oh, Baby Jesus grew.
He learned to walk
(Walk in place.)
Just like you do.
Oh, Baby Jesus grew.

Oh, Baby Jesus grew.
Oh, Baby Jesus grew.
He learned to run
(Run in place.)
Just like you do.
Oh, Baby Jesus grew.

Oh, Baby Jesus grew.
Oh, Baby Jesus grew.
He learned to hop
(Hop in place.)
Just like you do.
Oh, Baby Jesus grew.

Oh, Baby Jesus grew.
Oh, Baby Jesus grew.
He learned to pray
(Hold hands in prayer.)
Just like you do.
Oh, Baby Jesus grew.

Based on Luke 2:52
Words: Daphna Flegal
Words © 2001 Abingdon Press

In the Temple Courts
(Tune: The Pawpaw Patch)

Where, oh where, is our son Jesus?
Where, oh where, is our son Jesus?
Where, oh where, is our son Jesus?
We've been looking for him everywhere.

Here, oh here, is your son Jesus.
Here, oh here, is your son Jesus.
Here, oh here, is your son Jesus.
He is sitting in the Temple courts.

Based on Luke 2:41-52
Words: Daphna Flegal
Words © 2001 Abingdon Press

Jesus' Baptism

There Was a Man Named John
(Tune: The Farmer in the Dell)

There was a man named John.
There was a man named John.
He preached down by the riverside.
There was a man named John.

Oh, Jesus came to John.
Oh, Jesus came to John.
He went down by the riverside.
Oh, Jesus came to John.

"This is the Son of God."
"This is the Son of God."
John said down by the riverside,
"This is the Son of God."

Based on John 1:34
Words: Daphna Flegal
Words © 2001 Abingdon Press

Jesus Was Baptized
(Tune: Down by the Riverside)

I know that Jesus went to John,
Down by the riverside,
Down by the riverside,
Down by the riverside.
I know that Jesus went to John,
Down by the riverside,
Down by the riverside.

I know that Jesus was baptized,
Down by the riverside,
Down by the riverside,
Down by the riverside.
I know that Jesus was baptized,
Down by the riverside,
Down by the riverside.

I know a dove flew down from the sky,
Down by the riverside,
Down by the riverside,
Down by the riverside.
I know a dove flew down from the sky,
Down by the riverside,
Down by the riverside.

I know that Jesus is God's Son,
Down by the riverside,
Down by the riverside,
Down by the riverside.
I know that Jesus is God's Son,
Down by the riverside,
Down by the riverside.

Based on Luke 3:21-22
Words: Daphna Flegal
Words © 2001 Abingdon Press

J-E-S-U-S
(Tune: Bingo)

Jesus is the Son of God,
And I can spell his name-O.
J-E-S-U-S,
J-E-S-U-S,
J-E-S-U-S,
And Jesus is his name-O.

Jesus is the Son of God,
And I can spell his name-O.
(clap)-E-S-U-S,
(clap)-E-S-U-S,
(clap)-E-S-U-S,
And Jesus is his name-O.

Jesus is the Son of God,
And I can spell his name-O.
(clap)-(clap)-S-U-S,
(clap)-(clap)-S-U-S,
(clap)-(clap)-S-U-S,
And Jesus is his name-O.

Jesus is the Son of God,
And I can spell his name-O.
(clap)-(clap)-(clap)-U-S,
(clap)-(clap)-(clap)-U-S,
(clap)-(clap)-(clap)-U-S,
And Jesus is his name-O.

Jesus is the Son of God,
And I can spell his name-O.
(clap)-(clap)-(clap)-(clap)-S,
(clap)-(clap)-(clap)-(clap)-S,
(clap)-(clap)-(clap)-(clap)-S,
And Jesus is his name-O.

Jesus is the Son of God,
And I can spell his name-O.
(clap)-(clap)-(clap)-(clap)-(clap),
(clap)-(clap)-(clap)-(clap)-(clap),
(clap)-(clap)-(clap)-(clap)-(clap),
And Jesus is his name-O.

Jesus is the Son of God,
And I can spell his name-O.
J-E-S-U-S,
J-E-S-U-S,
J-E-S-U-S,
And Jesus is his name-O.

Based on John 1:34
Words: Cynthia Gray, Linda Ray Miller, and Fran Porter
Words © 2001 Cokesbury

Friends of Jesus

Four Fishermen
(Tune: London Bridge)

Jesus called four fishermen,
Fishermen, fishermen.
Jesus called four fishermen
To fish for people now.

I can fish for people too,
People too, people too.
I can fish for people too
And tell you God loves you.

Based on Luke 5:1-11
Words: Daphna Flegal
Words © 1998 Abingdon Press

Jesus Called Four Fishermen
(Tune: Twinkle, Twinkle, Little Star)

Jesus called four fishermen:
Peter, Andrew, James, and John.
"Follow me; for if you do,
You will fish for people too."
Jesus called four fishermen:
Peter, Andrew, James, and John.

Based on Luke 5:4-11
Words: Sharilyn S. Adair
Words © 1997 Cokesbury

Martha, Please Stop All Your Work
(Tune: Here We Go 'Round the Mulberry Bush)

Martha, please stop all your work,
All your work, all your work.
Martha, please stop all your work,
And sit down next to Jesus.

Based on Luke 10:38-42
Words: Daphna and Gary Flegal
Words © 2001 Abingdon Press

Martha's Song
(Tune: This Is the Way)

This is the way I sweep the house,
(Pretend to sweep.)
Sweep the house, sweep the house.
This is the way I sweep the house,
Getting ready for Jesus.

This is the way I cook the food,
(Pretend to stir a bowl of stew.)
Cook the food, cook the food.
This is the way I cook the food,
Getting ready for Jesus.

This is the way I talk to Mary,
(Shake index finger.)
Talk to Mary, talk to Mary.
This is the way I talk to Mary,
Getting ready for Jesus.

This is the way I sit and listen,
(Put hands in lap.)
Sit and listen, sit and listen.
This is the way I sit and listen,
Taking time for Jesus.

Based on Luke 10:38-42
Words: Daphna Flegal
Words © 2001 Abingdon Press

Matthew
(Tune: Are You Sleeping?)

"Matthew, Matthew,
Matthew, Matthew,
Come and see,
Come and see.
Leave everything and follow,
Leave everything and follow,
Follow me.
Follow me."

Based on Luke 5:27-28
Words: Daphna Flegal
Words © 2001 Abingdon Press

Zacchaeus
(Tune: Row, Row, Row Your Boat)

Up, up, up the tree,
(Pretend to climb up a tree.)
Zacchaeus climbed that day,
So he could see above the crowd
As Jesus passed that way.

Down, down, down the tree,
(Pretend to climb down a tree.)
Zacchaeus climbed that day.
'Cause Jesus said, "Zacch, come on down;
And at your house I'll stay."

Based on Luke 19:1-9
Words: Daphna Flegal
Words © 2001 Abingdon Press

Teachings of Jesus

Jesus Taught
(Tune: London Bridge)

Jesus taught about God's love.
(Fold hands over heart.)
Clap your hands; shout hooray!
(Clap; jab hand into air.)
Jesus taught about God's love.
(Fold hands over heart.)
We love Jesus.

Jesus taught about God's love.
(Fold hands over heart.)
Stomp your feet; shout hooray.
(Stomp; jab hand into air.)
Jesus taught about God's love.
(Fold hands over heart.)
We love Jesus.

Jesus taught about God's love.
(Fold hands over heart.)
Turn around; shout hooray.
(Turn around; jab hand into air.)
Jesus taught about God's love.
(Fold hands over heart.)
We love Jesus.

Based on Matthew 4:23-25
Words: Cynthia Gray
Words © 2000 Cokesbury

Jesus, Jesus, Hear My Prayer
(Tune: Twinkle, Twinkle, Little Star)

Jesus, Jesus, hear my prayer.
Help me love and help me share.
You are Teacher, Healer, Friend.
I know your love never ends.
Jesus, Jesus, hear my prayer.
I'm so glad that you are there.

Words: LeeDell Stickler
Words © 1997 Abingdon Press

Jesus Loves
(Tune: The Farmer in the Dell)

Yes, Jesus loves (*child's name*).
Yes, Jesus loves (*child's name*).
We know that Jesus is our friend,
Yes, Jesus loves (*child's name*).

Based on Mark 10:13-16
Words: Daphna Flegal
Words © 1997 Abingdon Press

Jesus Is a Friend of Mine
(Tune: Mary Had a Little Lamb)

Jesus is a friend of mine,
Friend of mine, friend of mine.
Jesus is a friend of mine.
He loves me all the time.

Based on John 15:15
Words: Daphna and Gary Flegal
Words © 2001 Abingdon Press

Miracles of Jesus

Jesus Is the Son of God
(Tune: Merrily We Roll Along)

Jesus is the Son of God,
Son of God, Son of God.
Jesus is the Son of God,
He came to show God's love.

Jesus can do miracles,
Miracles, miracles.
Jesus can do miracles,
He came to show God's love.

Jesus stopped the wind and waves,
Wind and waves, wind and waves.
Jesus stopped the wind and waves,
He came to show God's love.

Jesus said, "Stretch out your hand,
Out your hand, out your hand."
Jesus said, "Stretch out your hand."
He came to show God's love.

Jesus helped the men to see,
Men to see, men to see.
Jesus helped the men to see,
He came to show God's love.

Based on Matthew 8:23-26; 12:10-13; 20:29-34
Words: Cynthia Gray, Linda Ray Miller, and Fran Porter
Words © 2001 Cokesbury

He Can Do a Miracle
(Tune: If You're Happy and You Know It)

Oh, Jesus is God's Son, clap your hands
(*clap, clap*)
Oh, Jesus is God's Son, clap your hands
(*clap, clap*)
He can do a miracle, 'cause He's the Son
of God,
Oh, Jesus is God's Son, clap your hands.
(*clap, clap*)

Oh, Jesus is God's Son, stomp your feet
(*stomp, stomp*)
Oh, Jesus is God's Son, stomp your feet
(*stomp, stomp*)
He can do a miracle, 'cause He's the Son
of God,
Oh, Jesus is God's Son, stomp your feet.
(*stomp, stomp*)

Oh, Jesus is God's Son, shout hooray.
(*Hooray!*)
Oh, Jesus is God's Son, shout hooray.
(*Hooray!*)
He can do a miracle, 'cause He's the Son
of God,
Oh, Jesus is God's Son, shout hooray.
(*Hooray!*)

Based on John 1:34 (Good News Bible)
Words: Cynthia Gray, Linda Ray Miller, and Fran Porter
Words © 2001 Cokesbury

Now the Man Can See
(Tune: The Farmer in the Dell)

(Move hands over eyes.)
The blind man could not see.
The blind man could not see.
He sat beside the road all day.
The blind man could not see.

(Wipe hands together.)
Oh, Jesus made some mud.
Oh, Jesus made some mud.
He put it on the blind man's eyes.
Oh, Jesus made some mud.

(Pretend to wash face.)
"Go wash the mud away.
Go wash the mud away."
Jesus said, "Go to the pool;
go wash the mud away."

(Raise hands over head and move from side to side.)
And now the man could see.
And now the man could see.
The water washed the mud away;
and now the man could see.

Based on John 9:1-11
Words: Sharilyn S. Adair, Lora Jean Gowan, and Linda Ray Miller
Words © 2000 Cokesbury

The Boy's Lunch
(Tune: She'll Be Coming 'Round the Mountain)

Oh, Jesus taught the people all day long.
Oh, Jesus taught the people all day long.
From the morning to the evening,
From the morning to the evening,
Oh, Jesus taught the people all day long.

Oh, the people they were getting hungry now.
Oh, the people they were getting hungry now.
It was time to eat some supper,
It was time to eat some supper,
Oh, the people they were getting hungry now.

Oh, Jesus said to give the people food.
Oh, Jesus said to give the people food.
Then he turned to his disciples,
Then he turned to his disciples,
Oh, Jesus said to give the people food.

Then a boy said, "I will share my lunch with you."
Then a boy said, "I will share my lunch with you."
"I have barley loaves and fishes,
I have barley loaves and fishes."
Oh, a boy said, "I will share my lunch with you."

Oh, Jesus told the people to sit down.
Oh, Jesus told the people to sit down.
Then he thanked God for the fishes,
Then he thanked God for the fishes,
Oh, Jesus told the people to sit down.

Now everyone was fed from that small lunch.
Now everyone was fed from that small lunch.
Just two barley loaves and fishes,
Just two barley loaves and fishes,
Now everyone was fed from that small lunch.

Twelve baskets were left over from that lunch.
Twelve baskets were left over from that lunch.
After everyone had eaten,
After everyone had eaten,
Twelve baskets were left over from that lunch.

Based on John 6:1-14
Words: Daphna Flegal
Words © 2001 Abingdon Press

Holy Week

See Jesus Riding By
(Tune: Down by the Riverside)

We're gonna wave all our branches high!
(Pretend to wave palm branches.)
See Jesus riding by,
See Jesus riding by,
See Jesus riding by.
We're gonna wave all our branches high!
(Pretend to wave palm branches.)
See Jesus riding by,
See Jesus riding by.

We're gonna shout "Hosanna to our king!"
(Cup hands around mouth.)
See Jesus riding by,
See Jesus riding by,
See Jesus riding by.
We're gonna shout "Hosanna to our king!"

(Cup hands around mouth.)
See Jesus riding by,
See Jesus riding by.

We're gonna clap our hands and stomp our feet!
(Clap hands; stomp feet.)
See Jesus riding by,
See Jesus riding by,
See Jesus riding by.
We're gonna clap our hands and stomp our feet!
(Clap hands; stomp feet.)
See Jesus riding by,
See Jesus riding by.

Based on Mark 11:1-10
Words: Daphna Flegal
Words © 2001 Abingdon Press

Hosanna to the Son of God
(Tune: The Farmer in the Dell)

Oh, Jesus came to town.
(March in place.)
Oh, Jesus came to town.
(March in place.)
Hosanna to the Son of God!
(Wave one arm up high.)
Oh, Jesus came to town.
(March in place.)

He rode a little donkey.
(Pretend to ride donkey.)
He rode a little donkey.
(Pretend to ride donkey.)
Hosanna to the Son of God!
(Wave one arm up high.)
He rode a little donkey.
(Pretend to ride donkey.)

The people gathered 'round.
(March in place.)
The people gathered 'round.
(March in place.)
Hosanna to the Son of God!
(Wave one arm up high.)
The people gathered 'round.
(March in place.)

They waved their palms with joy.
(Wave both arms.)
They waved their palms with joy.
(Wave both arms.)
Hosanna to the Son of God!
(Wave one arm up high.)
They waved their palms with joy.
(Wave both arms.)

Oh, blessed is the king.
(Place hands over heart.)
Oh, blessed is the king.
(Place hands over heart.)
Hosanna to the Son of God!
(Wave one arm up high.)
Oh, blessed is the king.
(Place hands over heart.)

Based on Mark 11:1-10
Words: LeeDell Stickler
Words © 1998 Abingdon Press

Shout "Hosanna!"
(Tune: She'll Be Coming 'Round the Mountain)

He'll be riding on a donkey when he comes.
He'll be riding on a donkey when he comes.
He'll be riding on a donkey,
He'll be riding on a donkey,
He'll be riding on a donkey when he comes.

Oh, we'll all shout "Hosanna!" when he comes.
Oh, we'll all shout "Hosanna!" when he comes.
Oh, we'll all shout "Hosanna!"
Oh, we'll all shout "Hosanna!"
Oh, we'll all shout "Hosanna!" when he comes.

Based on Mark 11:1-10
Words: Daphna Flegal
Words © 1999 Abingdon Press

Garden of Gethsemane
(Tune: Are You Sleeping?)

Are you sleeping?
Are you sleeping?
(Fold your hands near your cheek.)
My good friends?
My good friends?
(Hold your hands over your heart.)
Now it's time to wake up!
Now it's time to wake up!
(Stretch arms above head.)
Pray with me.
Pray with me.
(Fold hands in prayer.)

Based on Matthew 26:36-46
Words: Sharilyn S. Adair, Lora Jean Gowan, and Linda Ray Miller
Words © 2000 Cokesbury

Bread and Juice
(Tune: Hot Cross Buns)

Bread and juice
Bread and juice
Jesus shared a special meal of
Bread and juice.

Bread and juice
Bread and juice
We remember Jesus with our
Bread and juice.

Based on Mark 14:12-16; 22-25
Words: Daphna Flegal
Words © 2001 Abingdon Press

Peter Heard the Rooster Crow
(Tune: Do You Know the Muffin Man?)

Peter, do you know this man,
Know this man, know this man?
Peter, do you know this man?
He is your friend.

No, I do not know this man,
Know this man, know this man.
No, I do not know this man.
He's not my friend.

Peter heard the rooster crow,
The rooster crow, the rooster crow.
Peter heard the rooster crow,
Cock-a-doodle-do!

Based on Luke 22:54-62
Words: Daphna Flegal
Words © 2001 Abingdon Press

Three Kind Friends
(Tune: Three Blind Mice)

Three kind friends,
Three kind friends,
Go to the tomb,
Go to the tomb.
They find the stone has been rolled away,
And Jesus is no longer there to stay.
He's alive on this first glad Easter day.
Oh, what great joy!
Oh, what great joy!

Based on Mark 16:1-7
Words: Sharilyn S. Adair
Words © 2001 Abingdon Press

This Special Day
(Tune: The Wheels on the Bus)

On this Easter day let's clap our hands,
(Clap hands.)
Clap our hands, clap our hands.
On this Easter day let's clap our hands,
For Jesus lives.

On this Easter day let's stomp our feet,
(Stomp feet.)
Stomp our feet, stomp our feet.
On this Easter day let's stomp our feet,
For Jesus lives.

On this Easter day let's turn around,
(Turn around.)
Turn around, turn around.
On this Easter day let's turn around,
For Jesus lives.

On this Easter day let's jump for joy,
(Jump in place.)
Jump for joy, jump for joy.
On this Easter day let's jump for joy,
For Jesus lives.

On this Easter day let's shout, "Hooray!"
(Cup hands around mouth.)
Shout, "Hooray," shout "Hooray!"
On this Easter day let's shout, "Hooray!"
For Jesus lives.

Based on Luke 24:1-10
Words: Daphna Flegal
Words © 2001 Abingdon Press

The Great Commission

I Can Tell
(Tune: This Old Man)

I can tell; you can tell,
(Point to self; point to others.)
With a whisper or a yell.
(Sing softly; sing loudly.)
Clap your hands and sing along with me.
(Clap hands.)
Jesus loves us all, you see!
(Fold hands over heart.)

I can tell; you can tell,
(Point to self; point to others.)
With a whisper or a yell.
(Sing softly; sing loudly.)
Stomp your feet and sing along with me.
(Stomp feet.)
Jesus loves us all, you see!
(Fold hands over heart.)

I can tell; you can tell,
(Point to self; point to others.)
With a whisper or a yell.
(Sing softly; sing loudly.)
Raise your arms and sing along with me.
(Raise arms.)
Jesus loves us all, you see!
(Fold hands over heart.)

I can tell; you can tell,
(Point to self; point to others.)
With a whisper or a yell.
(Sing softly; sing loudly.)
Tap your toes and sing along with me.
(Tap toes.)
Jesus loves us all, you see!
(Fold hands over heart.)

Based on Matthew 28:19-20
Words: Sharilyn S. Adair, Lora Jean Gowan, and
Linda Ray Miller
Words © 2000 Cokesbury

Tell of Jesus
(Tune: Are You Sleeping?)

Tell of Jesus, tell of Jesus,
Everywhere, everywhere.
We can be his helpers,
We can be his helpers,
Everywhere, everywhere.

Based on Matthew 28:19
Words: Sharilyn S. Adair
Words © 2000 Abingdon Press

Go to People Everywhere
(Tune: Twinkle, Twinkle, Little Star)

Go to people everywhere,
Tell them of my love and care.
Listen to these words I say,
I am with you everyday.
Go to people everywhere,
Tell them of my love and care.

Based on Matthew 28:19-20
Words: Daphna and Gary Flegal
Words © 2001 Abingdon Press

The First Christians

Pentecost Day
(Tune: She'll Be Coming 'Round the Mountain)

Oh, they were all together in one place.
Oh, they were all together in one place.
When the wind began a-blowing,
And the tongues of fire a-showing,
Oh, they were all together in one place.

And they knew God was with them all the time.
And they knew God was with them all the time.
Oh, they felt the Holy Spirit,
Oh, they felt the Holy Spirit,
And they knew God was with them all the time.

Oh, then Peter started preachin' to the crowd.
Oh, then Peter started preachin' to the crowd.
Oh, he told them about Jesus.
Oh, he told them about Jesus.
Oh, then Peter started preachin' to the crowd.

Oh, three thousand became Christians on that day.
Oh, three thousand became Christians on that day.
They were baptized as believers.
They were baptized as believers.
Oh, three thousand became Christians on that day.

Based on Acts 2:1-42
Words: Daphna Flegal
Words © 2001 Abingdon Press

The Man at the Gate
(Tune: The Wheels on the Bus)

The man at the gate said, "Help me, please,
(Hold out hand.)
"Help me, please; help me, please."
The man at the gate said, "Help me, please,
I cannot walk."

Peter and John said, "We've no gold,
(Shake head, no.)
"We've no gold; we've no gold."
Peter and John said, "We've no gold,
But we will help."

"In the name of Jesus, stand up and walk,
(Walk in place.)
"Up and walk, up and walk."
"In the name of Jesus, stand up and walk.
Stand up and walk."

The man at the gate stood up and walked,
(Walk in place.)
Up and walked, up and walked.
The man at the gate stood up and walked.
He was made strong.

The man at the gate jumped up and down,
(Jump in place.)
Jumped up and down, jumped up and down.
The man at the gate jumped up and down,
Shouting God's praise.

Based on Acts 3:1-10
Words: Daphna Flegal
Words © 2001 Abingdon Press

Dorcas Sews
(Tune: This Is the Way)

In and out the needle goes,
Needle goes, needle goes.
In and out the needle goes,
As Dorcas sews a robe.

Based on Acts 9:36-43
Words: Sharilyn S. Adair
Words © 2000 Cokesbury

First Christians
(Tune: Do You Know the Muffin Man?)

Oh, *(insert a child's name)* is a follower,
A follower, a follower.
Oh, *(insert name)* is a follower
Of Jesus, our friend.

Words: Sharilyn S. Adair, Lora Jean Gowan, and Linda Ray Miller
Words © 2000 Cokesbury

Paul and His Friends

Paul Was on the Road One Day
(Tune: Twinkle, Twinkle, Little Star)

Paul was on the road one day,
When he heard Lord Jesus say,
"Paul, why do you hurt my friends?
They know my love never ends.
Paul, believe I love you too;
I have work for you to do."

Based on Acts 9:1-9
Words: Daphna Flegal
Words © 2001 Abingdon Press

Lydia
(Tune: Do You Know the Muffin Man?)

Lydia sold purple cloth,
Purple cloth, purple cloth.
Lydia sold purple cloth,
Down in the town.

Lydia would pray to God,
Pray to God, pray to God.
Lydia would pray to God,
Down by the river.

Lydia met Paul one day,
Paul one day, Paul one day.
Lydia met Paul one day,
Down by the river.

He told her about God's Son,
About God's Son, about God's Son.
He told her about God's Son,
Jesus our friend.

She became a follower,
A follower, a follower.
She became a follower
Of Jesus, our friend.

Based on Acts 16:11-15
Words: Daphna Flegal
Words © 2001 Abingdon Press

Paul and His Friends
(Tune: She'll Be Coming 'Round the Mountain)

Oh, Paul and all his friends shared the good news.
Oh, Paul and all his friends shared the good news.
There was Timothy and Silas, and Aquila and Priscilla.
Oh, Paul and all his friends shared the good news.

Based on Acts: 15:40–16:3; 18:1-4
Words: Daphna Flegal
Words © 2001 Abingdon Press

Paul and Silas Went to Jail
(Tune: London Bridge)

Paul and Silas went to jail,
Went to jail, went to jail.
Paul and Silas went to jail.
The door was locked up tight.
(Make hands into fists; cross at wrists.)

When the ground began to shake,
Began to shake, began to shake,
When the ground began to shake,
The door was opened wide.
(Open arms wide.)

The jailer ran into the jail,
Into the jail, into the jail.
The jailer ran into the jail,
And found the two men.
(Make hands into fists; cross at wrists.)

Paul and Silas shared God's love,
Shared God's love, shared God's love.
Paul and Silas shared God's love
With the jailer.
(Cross hands over heart.)

Based on Acts 16:16-40
Words: Daphna Flegal
Words © 1999 Abingdon Press

Let's Go with Paul
(Tune: The Wheels on the Bus)

Oh, let's go with Paul and walk, walk, walk,
(Walk in place.)
Walk, walk, walk, walk, walk, walk.
Oh, let's go with Paul and walk, walk, walk,
To tell about Jesus.

Oh, let's go with Paul and march, march,
march,
(March in place.)
March, march, march, march, march,
march.
Oh, let's go with Paul and march, march,
march,
To tell about Jesus.

Oh, let's go with Paul and hop, hop, hop,
(Hop in place.)
Hop, hop, hop, hop, hop, hop.
Oh, let's go with Paul and hop, hop, hop,
To tell about Jesus.

Oh, let's go with Paul and tip, tiptoe,
(Tiptoe in place.)
Tip, tiptoe, tip, tiptoe.
Oh, let's go with Paul and tip, tiptoe,
To tell about Jesus.

Words: Daphna Flegal
Words © 2001 Abingdon Press

Praise

Ha, Ha!
(Tune: Boom Boom!)

Ha, ha! ain't it great to be happy!
Ha, ha! ain't it great to be happy!
Happy to know God loves us so;
Ha, ha! ain't it great to be happy!

Words: Daphna Flegal
Words © 2001 Abingdon Press

Praisin'
(Tune: Boom Boom!)

Clap, clap! *(Clap hands.)*
Ain't it great to be praisin',
Clap, clap! *(Clap hands.)*
Ain't it great to be praisin',
Praisin' the Lord with all our friends.
Clap, clap! *(Clap hands.)*
Ain't it great to be praisin'.

Stomp, stomp! *(Stomp feet.)*
Ain't it great to be praisin',
Stomp, stomp! *(Stomp feet.)*
Ain't it great to be praisin',
Praisin' the Lord with all our friends.
Stomp, stomp! *(Stomp feet.)*
Ain't it great to be praisin'.

Shake, shake! *(Shake hands with a
friend.)*
Ain't it great to be praisin',
Shake, shake! *(Shake hands.)*
Ain't it great to be praisin',
Praisin' the Lord with all our friends.
Shake, shake! *(Shake hands.)*
Ain't it great to be praisin'.

Bump, bump! *(Bump hips with a friend.)*
Ain't it great to be praisin',
Bump, bump! *(Bump hips with a friend.)*
Ain't it great to be praisin',
Praisin' the Lord with all our friends.
Bump, bump! *(Bump hips with a friend.)*
Ain't it great to be praisin'.

Words: Daphna Flegal
Words © 2001 Abingdon Press

Praise God All Day Long
(Tune: Row, Row, Row Your Boat)

Clap, clap, clap your hands
(Clap hands.)
And sing a happy song.
Stomp your feet and turn around.
(Stomp feet; turn around.)
Let's praise God all day long.

Words: Daphna Flegal
Words © 2001 Abingdon Press

Tell of God
(Tune: Twinkle, Twinkle, Little Star)

Tell of God to all your friends.
Tell them God's love never ends.
God is good and God is great.
Clap your hands and celebrate.
Tell of God to all your friends.
Tell them God's love never ends.

Words: Daphna and Diana Flegal
Words © 2001 Abingdon Press

Let's Praise the Lord
(Tune: The Wheels on the Bus)

Oh, let's praise the Lord and clap, clap, clap,
(Clap hands.)
Clap, clap, clap, clap, clap, clap.
Oh, let's praise the Lord and clap, clap, clap.
Let's praise the Lord!

Oh, let's praise the Lord and stomp, stomp, stomp,
(Stomp feet.)
Stomp, stomp, stomp, stomp, stomp, stomp.
Oh, let's praise the Lord and stomp, stomp, stomp.
Let's praise the Lord!

Oh, let's praise the Lord and pat, pat, pat,
(Pat knees.)
Pat, pat, pat, pat, pat, pat.
Oh, let's praise the Lord and pat, pat, pat.
Let's praise the Lord!

Oh, let's praise the Lord and hop, hop, hop,
(Hop up and down.)
Hop, hop, hop, hop, hop, hop.
Oh, let's praise the Lord and hop, hop, hop.
Let's praise the Lord!

Oh, let's praise the Lord and sit, sit, sit,
(Sit down.)
Sit, sit, sit, sit, sit, sit.
Oh, let's praise the Lord and sit, sit, sit.
Let's praise the Lord!

Words: Daphna Flegal
Words © 2001 Abingdon Press

Jump, Turn, Praise!
(Tune: Pick a Bale of Cotton)

Gonna jump down, turn around,
(Jump; turn around.)
Clap my hands and praise God.
(Clap hands; raise arms.)
Jump down, turn around,
(Jump; turn around.)
Clap my hands and praise!
(Clap hands; raise arms.)

Gonna jump down, turn around,
(Jump; turn around.)
Stomp my feet and praise God.
(Stomp feet; raise arms.)
Jump down, turn around,
(Jump; turn around.)
Stomp my feet and praise!
(Stomp feet, raise arms.)

Gonna jump down, turn around,
(Jump; turn around.)
Pat my head and praise God.
(Pat head; raise arms.)
Jump down, turn around,
(Jump; turn around.)
Pat my head and praise!
(Pat head; raise arms.)

Gonna jump down, turn around,
(Jump; turn around.)
Swing my hips and praise God.
(Swing hips; raise arms.)
Jump down, turn around,
(Jump; turn around.)
Swing my hips and praise!
(Swing hips; raise arms.)

Gonna jump down, turn around,
(Jump; turn around.)
Shake my self and praise God.
(Wiggle whole body; raise arms.)
Jump down, turn around,
(Jump; turn around.)
Shake my self and praise!
(Wiggle whole body; raise arms.)

Words: Daphna Flegal
Words © 2001 Abingdon Press

I've Been Working on the Railroad

MUSIC: Traditional

I'm a Little Teapot

MUSIC: Traditional

Three Blind Mice

MUSIC: Traditional

Here We Go 'Round the Mulberry Bush

MUSIC: Traditional

The Itsy Bitsy Spider

MUSIC: Traditional

Old MacDonald

MUSIC: Traditional

God Is So Good

MUSIC: Traditional

If You're Happy and You Know It

MUSIC: Traditional

Baa, Baa, Black Sheep

MUSIC: Traditional

Hot Cross Buns

MUSIC: Traditional

Down by the Bay

MUSIC: Traditional

Did You Ever See a Lassie?

MUSIC: Traditional

London Bridge

MUSIC: Traditional

The More We Get Together

MUSIC: Traditional

This Old Man

MUSIC: Traditional

Do You Know the Muffin Man?

MUSIC: Traditional

She'll Be Coming 'Round the Mountain

MUSIC: Traditional

Bingo

MUSIC: Traditional

Down by the Riverside

MUSIC: Traditional

The Farmer in the Dell

MUSIC: Traditional

Row, Row, Row Your Boat

MUSIC: Traditional

My Bonnie Lies over the Ocean

MUSIC: Traditional

The Wheels on the Bus

MUSIC: Traditional

Twinkle, Twinkle Little Star

MUSIC: Traditional

Are You Sleeping?

MUSIC: Traditional

Mary Had a Little Lamb

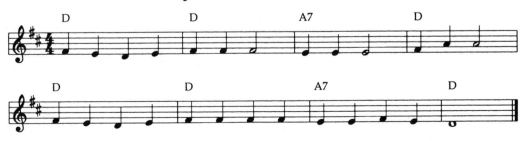

MUSIC: Traditional

Merrily We Roll Along

MUSIC: Traditional

This Is the Way

MUSIC: Traditional

The Pawpaw Patch

MUSIC: Traditional

Pick a Bale of Cotton

MUSIC: Traditional

In a Cabin in a Wood

MUSIC: Traditional

Boom Boom!

MUSIC: Traditional

Index of Titles

Index of Tunes